32

Christopher Columbus

and the Discovery of the New World

Explorers of New Worlds

Christopher Columbus

and the Discovery of the New World

Carole S. Gallagher

Chelsea House Publishers
Philadelphia

Prepared for Chelsea House Publishers by:
OTTN Publishing, Warminster, PA

CHELSEA HOUSE PUBLISHERS
Editor in Chief: Stephen Reginald
Managing Editor: James D. Gallagher
Production Manager: Pamela Loos
Art Director: Sara Davis
Director of Photography: Judy L. Hasday
Senior Production Editor: LeeAnne Gelletly
Series Designer: Keith Trego

3 5 7 9 8 6 4 2

Library of Congress Cataloging-in-Publication Data

Gallagher, Carole S.
    Christopher Columbus and the discovery of the New
    World / by Carole S. Gallagher
p.   cm. – (Explorers of new worlds)
Includes bibliographical references and index.
Summary: A biography of the Italian explorer who, in
the fifteenth century, became the first European to discover the West Indies islands, located below the south-
ernmost tip of the United States, in four historic voyages
sponsored by Spain's monarchy.
ISBN 0-7910-5509-4 (hc)
1. Columbus, Christopher–Juvenile literature. 2. Explorers–America–Biography Juvenile literature. 3. Explorers–Spain–Biography Juvenile literature. 4. America–
Discovery and exploration–Spanish Juvenile literature.
[1. Columbus, Christopher. 2. Explorers. 3. America–
Discovery and exploration–Spanish.] I. Title. II. Series.
E111.C15   1999
970.01'5–dc21   99-22256
                                                        CIP

Contents

Christopher Columbus is greeted by Queen Isabella at the Spainish court after his successful voyage to the East Indies. It was not until years later that people realized Columbus had found a new world.

Moment of Triumph

I

On March 13, 1493, a small ship called the *Niña* arrived at the port city of Palos. Seven and a half months earlier, the *Niña*'s captain, Christopher Columbus, had left this port in southern Spain with two other ships. Now, he was returning in triumph. Columbus had done what most people felt was impossible. He had reached the East Indies by sailing west.

The story of Columbus's fantastic voyage were already known when the *Niña* landed in Spain. He had sent a message ahead from Lisbon, the capital of Portugal, where the *Niña* had been forced to stop for repairs on the way home.

Columbus reported that he had found a sea route to the Indies and claimed islands there for Spain.

News about the discovery spread quickly. The King and Queen had ordered the letter to be copied and distributed throughout the land. When Columbus came ashore at Palos, along with natives of the islands he had found, he was Spain's grandest hero.

Columbus soon received a summons from Ferdinand and Isabella to visit them at the royal court. He was also told to plan for a second voyage. The letter was addressed to the "Admiral of the Ocean Sea, Viceroy and Governor of the islands that he hath discovered in the Indies." These titles had been promised to Columbus if his voyage succeeded. Their use told him that the king and queen intended to honor their agreement. The sailor quickly set out for Barcelona, on the opposite side of Spain.

The journey was a triumphant procession. Columbus "set out in the finest clothing he possessed, taking the Indians with him," wrote a man who lived at that time named Bartolomé Las Casas. The Admiral brought many gifts for the king and queen: colorful green parrots, masks and belts made from fishbones and decorated with pearls and gold, and samples of the finest native gold work.

As he traveled, the people of Spain came out to cheer. "As the news began to spread . . . that new lands called the Indies with a large and varied population had been discovered, as well as other things, and that the person who discovered them was coming on such-and-such a road, bringing those people with him, not only did everyone in the towns along his route turn out to see him, but many towns far from his route were emptied," wrote Las Casas.

In Barcelona, people crowded the streets to see Columbus pass. When he entered the courtyard of the Alcázar, a splendid palace built centuries earlier, the nobles stood in his honor. In the great throne room, Columbus knelt at the feet of Ferdinand and Isabella and kissed their hands as a sign of respect. Sitting beside the king and queen, and their son Prince Juan, Columbus told about his adventures. He introduced the six Indians, representatives of the island's Taino tribe. They wanted to become Christians, Columbus said. The welcoming ceremony ended with a prayer of thanksgiving.

For weeks Columbus was honored at public parties and private banquets. The Indians were baptized as Christians, with King Ferdinand and Prince Juan acting as godfathers. The king and queen also made good on their agreement with Columbus. He received a house in the town of Seville. Columbus was granted a **coat of arms**, and Ferdinand and Isabella permitted him to use their royal symbols, a lion and a castle, in his design. The other symbols the sailor chose were islands, which represented his discoveries, and anchors, reflecting his new title as Admiral of the Ocean Sea. At Columbus's request, his brothers Bartholomeo and Diego were also given noble titles.

The king and queen were very grateful to Columbus. By finding a western sea route to the East Indies, he had given them an advantage over Portugal. Portugal was a small country on the border of Spain. The Portuguese operated profitable trade routes to the south. For many years, they had been trying to find the Orient by sailing around the tip of Africa and heading east.

Ocean routes to the East Indies were important. Land travel from Europe to Asia was dangerous, difficult, and took a long time. However, many Europeans wanted goods that could be found only in the East Indies. Items like silk cloth and **spices** that were used to flavor and preserve meat were very valuable. Because they were so hard to get, the nation

The symbols on Christopher Columbus's coat of arms represented his accomplishment. At the top were the royal symbols of Ferdinand and Isabella, a castle and a lion. On the lower left, Columbus placed a group of islands and anchors.

that found a way to trade directly for them would become incredibly rich.

For many frustrating years, Columbus had tried to organize a voyage to the East Indies. He believed that by sailing west, he would land in Cathay (as China was known in Columbus's time) or Cipango (the islands of Japan). He had dared to sail the unknown distance of the **Ocean Sea**, as the Atlantic Ocean was then called, and he had succeeded. It was not until years later that people realized Columbus had not found the East Indies. The islands he had discovered were off the coast of a unknown continent—the New World.

The Spirit of
Exploration

This picture of the busy harbor of Genoa was painted when Christopher Columbus was a young man. Genoa is an Italian city on the Mediterranean Sea. Ships from all over Europe came to Genoa during the 15th and 16th centuries, bringing exotic goods from faraway lands.

2

Christopher Columbus was born in Genoa, Italy. The exact date is not known, but it was probably in late summer or early fall of 1451. If he followed the customs of his time, he probably celebrated his birthday on June 25th, the feast day of his patron saint, St. Christopher.

Cristoforo (his name in Italian) was the first child of Domenico and Susanna Colombo. Domenico and Susanna were wool weavers. They married in about 1445, and rented a house just inside the Porta dell'Olivella, the eastern gate of Genoa. It was in this house that Christoforo was born and lived until he was four. He had a younger sister, Bianchineta, and a younger brother, Giovanni. Two other brothers, Bartholomeo, born two years after Christoforo, and Diego, 17 years younger, would one day join in his explorations.

Young Christoforo was not able to go to school. He was needed to work in the family business. Because of this, he grew up without learning how to read or write.

From childhood, Columbus was attracted by the sea, the center of life in Genoa. Ships were built along the shore. Great trading vessels were constantly coming and going. In later years, Columbus wrote in a letter that he "entered upon the sea sailing" at a "very tender age." He was probably around 14 years old. It would have been natural for Domenico to send his teenage son on short journeys to sell his cloth and buy wool in the towns along the coast of the Mediterranean sea.

When he grew older, Columbus began to earn his living as a sailor. He learned important skills: how to steer, estimate distances, handle the sails, and other elements of seamanship.

Perhaps Columbus first developed his interest in the sea while looking at the thriving harbor of Genoa through this window in his house.

In August 1476, Columbus shipped out as a sailor on the *Bechalla*. This was one of five Genoese ships taking goods to England and Flanders. He was 25, and until now all of his sailing had been in the Mediterranean Sea. This trip would be on the open waters of the Ocean Sea.

The voyage turned into a disaster when the convoy was attacked by 13 French pirate ships. A battle raged all day. When the pirates tried to board, desperate sailors heaved pots of blazing **pitch** at their decks and rigging to set them on fire. The ships were so close together that flames spread to the merchant ships as well. By nightfall, four pirate ships and three of the Genoese vessels had sunk, including the *Bechalla.* Many sailors were drowned. Columbus, who was an excellent swimmer, grasped a piece of wreckage. Clinging to it, he started swimming toward the shore, six miles away. Eventually, he crawled out of the waves onto a beach in Portugal.

When Columbus had recovered from this ordeal, he visited Lisbon, the capital of Portugal. Many people from Genoa had moved to Lisbon. Among them was his brother Bartholomeo, who was working as a mapmaker.

At this time, Portugal was more actively engaged in exploration by sea than any other nation in Europe. A Portuguese leader named Prince Henry the Navigator had established a school to teach sailing skills. He also sent expeditions south along the coast of Africa. His shipbuilders designed a new type of ship, called a **caravel**. Mediterranean ships were large so that they could carry large quantities of trade goods. The caravel was smaller and easier to steer. Many great explorers would make their voyages of discovery on caravels.

Columbus became caught up in the spirit of exploration. He was eager for knowledge, and taught himself how to read and write in Portuguese and Spanish. (Both of these languages were used in Lisbon.) He read the Bible. He also studied books on *geography* that had been written by ancient Greeks and Arabs. He was learning more about sailing and the sea, also. Columbus made voyages to the Azores, Iceland, and Ireland.

In Lisbon, he met a woman named Felipa

In the late 1470s, Columbus sailed to Ireland. In the Irish port of Galway, he saw two dead bodies that had washed ashore. Their faces looked so different that people believed the bodies had floated from China.

Perestrelle e Moniz at church. They fell in love, and were married in 1479, when he was 28 years old. She called her husband Christoveo. (This is Portuguese for Christopher.)

Felipa's father had been a sea captain and explorer. He had helped discover a group of small islands 60 miles southwest of Portugal off the coast of Africa. These islands were called the Madeiras.

No one is sure exactly what Columbus looked like—all the portraits of him were made after his death. Columbus's son Ferdinand described him as "a well-built man . . . his body neither fat nor lean. He had an aquiline nose and light-colored eyes; the complexion pale, tending to bright red; the beard and hair, when he was a youth, fair, but which soon became gray."

Before his death, Felipa's father had been governor of a Portuguese colony on the Madeira island of Porto Santo. When Felipa's mother heard that Columbus was interested in sailing and exploration, she gave him her husband's maps, logs, and sailing charts. These contained valuable information about the Ocean Sea.

Christoveo and Felipa decided to make their home in Madeira, the largest of the islands. They soon had a son, Diego. Columbus continued to sail, learning more about *navigation* and ship handling in open waters. By 1483, he was no longer content to sail to places chosen by others. He had a new idea for a voyage of exploration that he was certain would be successful.

The Portuguese believed that if they could sail around the southern tip of Africa, they could reach the Indies by heading east. However, Portuguese sailors had explored 5,000 miles of the African coast without finding the tip. There seemed to be no end in sight. Columbus had a different solution. He proposed sailing west across the Ocean Sea. All educated people agreed that the earth was round, so by sailing west one must eventually come to the East, he argued. What was uncertain was how long the journey would take and whether the Indies could be reached before food ran out.

Columbus was convinced that the distance was not too far to be reached by a skilled mariner like himself. He found support for his idea in the Bible and other religious writings. For example, a passage in one religious source read, "And on the third day, [God] united the waters and the earth's seventh part, and dried the other six parts." Columbus thought this meant that the world was made of six parts land and one part water. If that was so, then the Ocean Sea between Europe and Asia could not be very large.

After the Bible, Columbus's chief source was *Imago Mundi* (Image of the World). This was a collection of writings about geography. He was greatly influenced, too, by *The Book of Marco Polo*, which recounted the adventures of a young traveler from Venice in the Orient two centuries before.

As he researched his theory, Columbus learned about someone else who had come up with a similar idea. In 1474 an Italian doctor, mathematician, and geographer named Paolo Toscanelli dal Pozzo had written to the king of Portugal, urging him to sponsor a westward expedition to the Indies.

Toscanelli even included a detailed map of his proposed route. Columbus wrote to Toscanelli, who sent him a copy of the letter and map.

Using the writings that supported his theory that the Ocean Sea was small, Columbus made calculations. The distance across the Ocean Sea, he decided, was about 2,400 **nautical miles**. (A nautical mile is a measurement of distance over water. It is about 800 feet longer than a mile on land.) He measured from the Canary Islands, west of Portugal, to Cipango, where he expected to land. (These numbers are wrong—the distance is actually more than 10,000 nautical miles. And, of course, Columbus didn't realize that there was a continent between Europe and China!)

In 1483 or 1484, Columbus and his family returned from Madeira to Lisbon. There, he asked King João II to sponsor his voyage. The king turned down his request. At around the same time, Felipa died. Grieving, and in need of a fresh start, Columbus and his son Diego went to Spain.

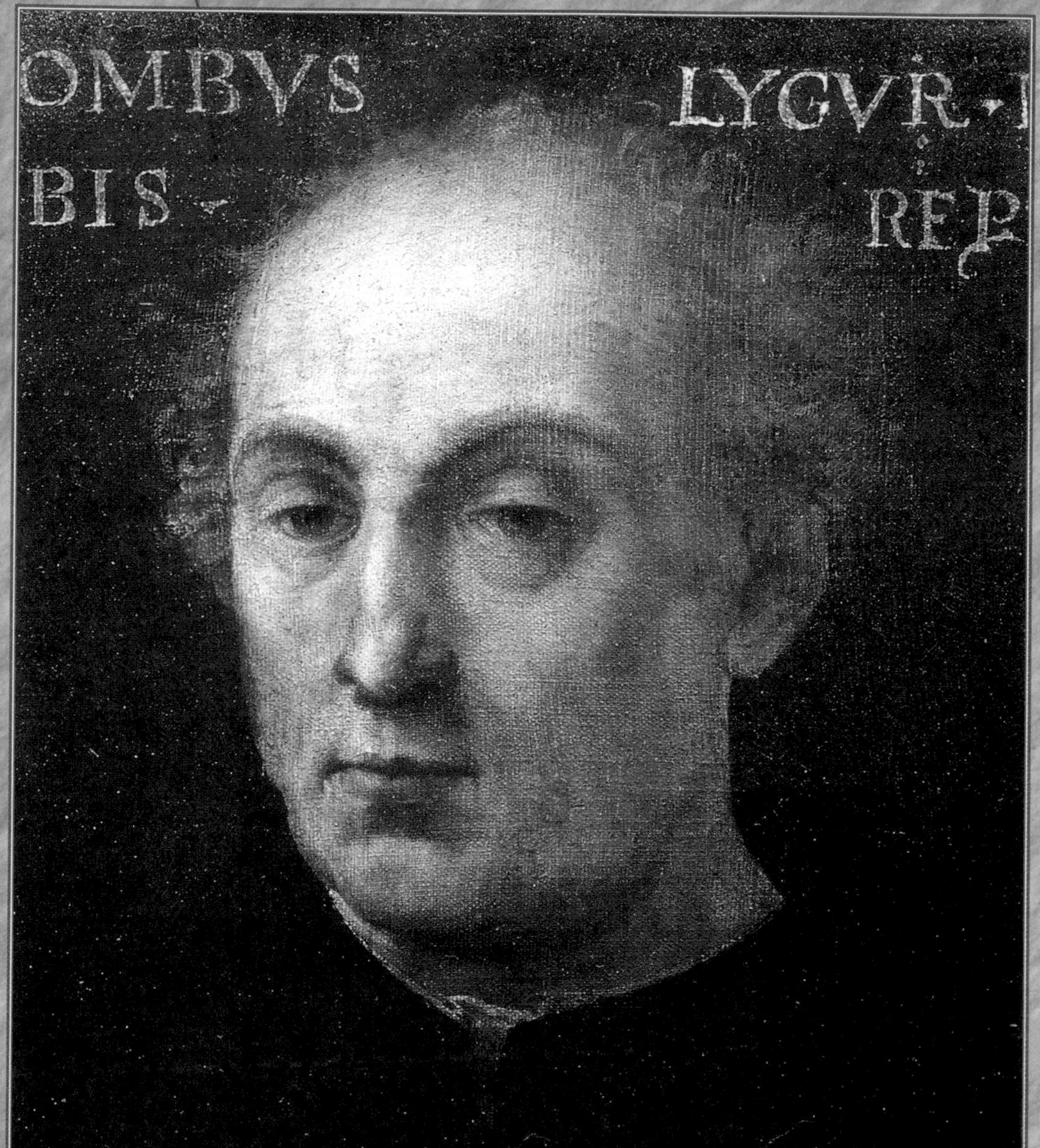
OMBVS
LYGVR.
BIS
REP

Christopher Columbus looks serious in this portrait. Perhaps he is reflecting over the many difficult years in which he attempted to convince people that his plan to reach the Indies by sailing west would work.

The Years of Great Anguish

3

he first stop for Christopher and Diego Columbus was Palos, a Spanish port near the border of Portugal. Two of Felipa's sisters lived nearby with their families. As the ship carrying Columbus and his son sailed up the Tinto River, it passed a **monastery** called La Rabida. Christopher and Diego walked from the dock to the monastery, which was located on a bluff above the ocean.

At La Rabida, Columbus met Friar Antonio Marchena, a well-educated priest, and the monastery's **rector**, Friar Juan Pérez.

Columbus had moved to Spain hoping to find a rich

man who could pay for a westward voyage to the Indies. But no one could help him unless the king and queen gave permission. When Queen Isabella of Spain heard about Columbus's unusual proposal to reach the Indies, she sent for the Genoese sailor.

At this time, Spain had no fixed capital city. Ferdinand and Isabella traveled around the country to oversee its affairs. Columbus went to a city called Córdoba and waited for the king and queen to arrive. Although the waiting was frustrating, there were good times too. Columbus fell in love with a woman named Beatriz Enriquez de Harana. Beatriz and Christopher had a son they named Ferdinand.

When the court arrived, Columbus was invited to meet King Ferdinand and Queen Isabella. The queen took a liking to Columbus at this first meeting. They were about the same age. Isabella also shared Columbus's interest in finding the Indies, and his desire to spread Christianity to the **heathens** in other parts of the world.

But even though Isabella liked Columbus, the queen did not immediately agree to pay for his voyage. Instead, she asked a group of her advisors to look into Columbus's proposal. This committee of priests and scholars was headed by Bishop Talavera.

Columbus later called the period that followed "the years of great anguish." He had to follow the Talavera commission from one city to another, waiting for their decision. Although Columbus had complete faith in himself and his idea, he had no proof that it could be done. He did not even have solid facts that he could use to explain or argue. Columbus simply insisted, over and over, that he knew he could do it. As months turned into years, he became a joke at court.

In 1490, after six years of study, the Talavera commission recommended that the king and queen reject Columbus's proposal. The scholars believed—correctly, as it turned out—that the distance between Europe and Asia was much greater than Columbus's estimate. Also, they felt that there were no new islands to discover in the west.

A disappointed Christopher Columbus returned to Palos. His friends Friar Pérez and Friar Marchena cheered him up. Friar Pérez asked Columbus not to leave Spain. The priest also spoke with Queen Isabella. He convinced the queen to let Columbus present his plan again.

In late December 1491, Christopher Columbus visited the king and queen again. This time, the committee of scholars also included Spain's financial managers. These men would decide whether supporting Columbus's voyage would be profitable.

Columbus's plan for the voyage was the same, but he changed his proposal. Before, he had begged for a few ships and supplies. This time, Columbus set a high price for undertaking the "Enterprise of the Indies," as he called it. If he succeeded, he wanted the title Admiral of the Ocean Sea. He wanted to be placed in charge of any new lands he claimed for Spain. He wanted these titles to be **hereditary**, meaning they would be passed on to his children and grandchildren. And, he wanted a tenth of all riches gained from the new lands.

Ferdinand and Isabella were ready to reconsider Columbus's proposal, but his new demands annoyed them. They refused to help him. Rejected again, Columbus set off on his mule. He intended to leave Spain and seek support elsewhere.

After the sailor left, King Ferdinand's treasurer Luis de Santangel suggested that the king and queen reconsider. The expedition would cost very little, he reminded the rulers. And if Columbus did succeed, Spain would gain so much wealth that the sailor would have earned the riches he asked for. Finally,

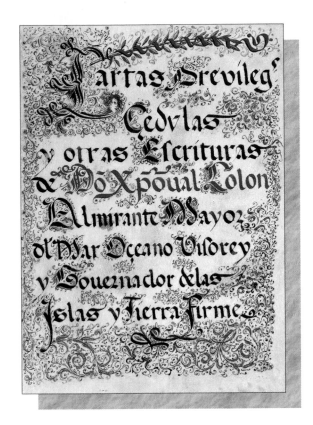

An ornate page from the agreement, or Capitulations, between Columbus and the king and queen of Spain

he pointed out that Spain would lose a great deal if Columbus succeeded while sailing for another country. That convinced the queen to change her mind.

Columbus was riding down the Córdoba road when Isabella's messenger caught up to him with a request that he return to court. After several months of bargaining, a contract called the ***Capitulations***, from the Spanish word for chapters (capítulos), was signed. This agreement gave Columbus all he had asked for. At last, he would have the opportunity to prove that he was right.

Thirty-Three
Days at Sea

On the 500th anniversary of Christopher Columbus's voyage, these replicas of his tiny caravels recreated the famous journey. Can you imagine what life must have been like on the cramped ships? In the background, the vessel of modern-day explorers can be seen— the space shuttle Discovery *on its launch pad.*

4

On May 23, 1492, Ferdinand and Isabella ordered the townspeople of Palos to give Columbus two ships for his voyage. The city provided the caravels *Niña* and *Pinta* for Columbus. The sailor also decided to rent a larger ship from a man named Juan de la Cosa. Columbus renamed the ship *Santa María*.

Columbus was lucky to get a good crew. Martín Alonso Pinzón, who was considered the finest sailor in Palos, agreed to join his voyage. Pinzón himself recruited the best sailors, telling them that in the East Indies they would find palaces, jewels, and gold. The crew totaled 90 men, including Columbus. It also included a man who spoke Arabic. If the ships reached Cathay, he might be able to talk with the ruler that Marco Polo had called the Grand Khan. There was also a secretary on board, whose job was to keep a list of new territories that Columbus discovered for Spain. He would also write down any agreements that were made with other rulers. Columbus carried letters from Ferdinand and Isabella to give to the Grand Khan.

Martín Pinzón would command the *Pinta,* which carried a crew of 26 men. His brother, Francisco, was the ship's master, or second in command. Francisco Pinzón was in charge of the crew, sails and rigging. The *Niña*'s captain was another brother, Vicente Yáñez Pinzón, and the ship's owner, Juan Niño, was master of the 24-man crew. Columbus would direct all of the ships from the *Santa María,* and Juan de la Cosa was hired as the **flagship**'s master, overseeing the crew of 40.

By the beginning of August, everything was ready. On the last night ashore, the crew went to

Columbus says farewell to his friends Friar Marchena and Friar Pérez as he prepares to leave Palos in the Santa María *on August 3, 1492.*

church. Shortly before dawn on Friday, August 3, 1492, they set sail.

The small fleet's first stop was the Canary Islands. This small group of islands is off the coast of Africa. In the Canary Islands, **provisions** were brought on board the caravels. Also, the rudder of the *Pinta*, which had broken on the way, was repaired. On September 9, Columbus's ships left the Canaries and headed west.

As the days passed, the crew grew uneasy. As they sailed farther into the unknown waters of the Ocean Sea, the superstitious sailors remembered stories about sea monsters, boiling seas, and whirlpools. In mid-September, they reached the **Sargasso Sea**. This calm water was covered with green algae that looked like grass. Some sailors were afraid that the ships would get tangled in the seaweed, but Columbus ordered them to sail ahead.

Columbus's decision to sail south to the Canary Islands, then turn west, was smart. By doing this, he took advantage of strong winds, known as the *trade winds*. These would push his ships across the Ocean Sea faster. The ships made excellent time, sometimes covering nearly 200 miles a day.

The caravels' speed slowed now, and sometimes there was an opposing wind. "This head wind was utterly indispensable to me," Columbus wrote in his log, "because my sailors by now must have been quite worked up against me, thinking that there were no winds capable of bringing me back to Spain." He was not worried, for he knew that to the north of his course gusted westerly winds that could take them home.

When the ships sailed into an area where there had been recent storms, they were surrounded by 100-foot waves. In his journal, Columbus noted his belief that God was protecting them as they sailed through the storm unharmed. October arrived and flocks of sea birds flying over were the only hopeful sign that a shore might be near. At sunset on October 7, Columbus saw a large flock of birds flying southwest. He decided to adjust his course slightly to follow the migrating birds.

On the afternoon of October 11, 33 days after the caravels had left the Canary Islands, the sailors noticed branches with flowers floating in the water. Now they were certain land was near. At sunset, Columbus spotted a glow on the horizon. He later wrote that it appeared to be "a little wax candle bobbing up and down." Although one other crewman also saw the light, most others did not. However, the crews of all three ships kept looking for land through the night.

As the caravels continued into unknown waters, some of the frightened sailors asked Columbus to turn the ships around, but he refused. The crews threatened to take over control of the ships, but they knew they needed Columbus's knowledge of the sea in order to return home. On October 9, 1492, Columbus agreed to turn back if land was not spotted within the next three or four days. Two days later, land was discovered.

At two o'clock in the morning, a sailor on the *Pinta* shouted, "Land! Land!" He had noticed a white beach in the moonlight. Martín Pinzón fired one of his ship's cannons. This was a signal to the other ships that land had been spotted.

The ships stayed offshore until morning, when a safe harbor could be found. Columbus was worried that **coral reefs** might damage his ships. These are large underwater ridges made up of the stony skeletons of sea creatures called coral. The reefs are very hard, and have sharp edges that can rip holes in the *hull* of a wooden ship.

After daybreak on October 12, Columbus found a harbor and anchored his ships. A landing party set out for shore in the ships' small boats. It included Columbus and his captains, Martín and Vicente Pinzón; the fleet secretary, Rodrigo de Escobedo; and the expedition's treasurer, Rodrigo Sanchez. When they landed on the beach, the party unfurled the royal banner of Spain, and flags with the symbols of Ferdinand and Isabella.

Columbus led the group in a prayer of thanksgiving. Next, he claimed the island for Spain. He erected a cross and named the island San Salvador (Holy Savior). Some curious natives of the island approached the Spaniards during the ceremony.

Columbus's first concern was to find out where he was. Marco Polo, Toscanelli, and the other scholars he had studied all said there were many islands off the coast of Cathay. Taking Indians with him as guides, he went from one island to the next, naming and claiming them for Spain.

The natives were friendly but poor. Columbus and his sailors had been expecting to find great riches. But every place they visited, the inhabitants said the gold was on the next island. At one village Columbus visited, he heard the natives talk about a city called Cubanacan. He thought this word meant Grand Khan—the mighty ruler of the East Indies that Marco Polo had written about. But when he arrived, Cubanacan turned out to be a town of 500 huts.

One day the *Pinta* disappeared. Martín Pinzón had decided to go on his own to an island where there was rumored to be gold. Columbus was very angry, but he decided to continue exploring instead of chasing the *Pinta*.

Finally, Columbus arrived at the island he called *la Isla Española* (the Spanish Isle). It later became known as Hispaniola. He was delighted by the island's beauty. Describing it later to Ferdinand and Isabella, he wrote, "There were singing the nightingale and other little birds of a thousand kinds in the month of November, there where I went. There are palm trees of six or eight kinds, which are a wonder to behold on account of their beautiful variety, and so are the other trees and fruits and herbs; . . . . There are many spices and great mines of gold and of other metals."

The Indians on Hispaniola did have some gold, and they were willing to exchange it. The ships

The Spaniards were fascinated by the natives that they found in the New World. "We saw naked people," Columbus wrote. "All those that I saw were young people, for none did I see of more than thirty years of age. They are all very well formed, with handsome bodies and good faces. Their hair [is] coarse, almost like the tail of a horse–and short. They wear their hair down over their eyebrows except for a little in back which they wear long and never cut."

Columbus called them "Indios," because he believed they were natives of the Indies. As a result the term "Indians" has been used to describe the native peoples of North and South America.

sailed along the coast and anchored each night so that the natives could come out to visit and trade.

On December 24, the ships were sailing around Hispaniola so that Columbus could meet a native chief named Guacanagari. The chief had sent Columbus a gold belt, and the sailor hoped to befriend Guacanagari and find his source of gold.

Even though they were sailing through danger-ous shoreline waters, an inexperienced boy was in charge of steering the boat after 11 P.M. He didn't do a very good job. The *Santa María* ran aground on a coral reef. The ship's hull was damaged beyond repair. The Indians helped the sailors move all of the supplies to the *Niña.*

With only one ship left, Columbus could not risk further exploration. "I recognized that our Lord has caused me to run aground at this place," he wrote, "so that I might establish a settlement here." Using wood from the wreck of the *Santa María,* the sailors built a fort. Because it was Christmas, they called the fort Navidad (the Nativity). Thirty-nine men volun-teered to stay behind and try to find gold. The rest crowded onto the *Niña* for the voyage back to Spain. They brought along six of the Indians to show King Ferdinand and Queen Isabella.

The *Niña* departed on January 4, 1493. After two days at sea, the *Pinta* was sighted. When the ships came together, Pinzón went aboard the *Niña* and apologized. He had not found gold. Columbus no longer trusted him, but he welcomed Pinzón back.

The ships sailed together until mid-February, when they were separated by a terrible storm that lasted for three days. The weather was so fierce that even Columbus feared his ship would be lost. Later, a second storm tore the sails from the masts. Fortunately, the *Niña* was now near the coast of Portugal, so Columbus stopped at Lisbon for repairs. There, he wrote to the king and queen about his discovery.

The *Niña* sailed into the harbor at Palos on March 15, 1493. The *Pinta* had landed in northern Spain a few weeks earlier. Martín Pinzón sent word to Ferdinand and Isabella. He asked permission to come at once to court. They told him to wait for Columbus's return, preventing him from stealing the glory. Upon arriving in Spain, Martín Pinzón went home. He died within the month.

As for Columbus, he was a national hero. Ferdinand and Isabella publicly honored the Admiral of the Ocean Sea. At last, his vision, courage, and skill were recognized and rewarded.

Columbus was a hero when he returned to Spain in 1492. However, finding Hispaniola turned out to be much easier than ruling the Spanish colony that he established there.

Admiral of the Mosquitoes 5

I t was easy for Christopher Columbus to find sailors for his second voyage. Many people wanted to see the Indies—and perhaps become rich there! On September 25, 1493, Columbus's fleet of 17 ships, carrying 1,200 men, set out from Palos.

Columbus intended to explore until he found the Grand Khan. But in order to profit from the lands he had discovered, it was necessary for him to establish a colony. He was given authority to rule. The ships carried soldiers to conquer the Indians, priests to convert them to Christianity, farmers, guard dogs, and farm animals.

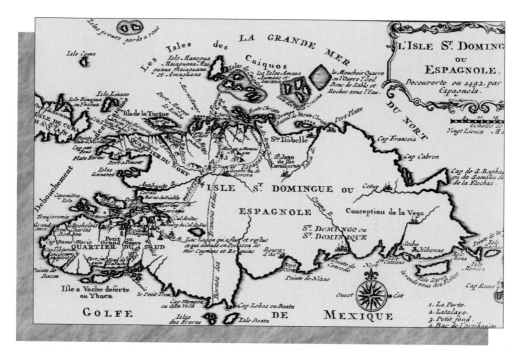

This old map shows the island of Hispaniola, where Columbus's first settlement was established. The Spaniards also settled on nearby Cuba and Puerto Rico.

Upon reaching Hispaniola on November 23, 1493, the first men to go ashore found two dead Spaniards tied to a tree. Columbus quickly sailed on to Navidad. The fleet arrived at nightfall four days later. Signal torches and cannon shots from the ships were not answered from shore. The darkness and silence filled the travelers with dread. In the morning, Navidad was found to be a charred ruin. The corpses of the Spaniards were scattered for miles and there were no survivors.

Messengers from Guacanagari told Columbus what had happened. After the Admiral had left Navidad, the Spaniards who stayed behind became greedy. Some raided the nearby Indian villages, taking gold and women. In return, an Indian chief named Caonabo began to ambush them. Then he led an attack on the fort and killed the remaining men. This discovery destroyed Columbus's hopes for peace between the Indians and Spanish. It also shocked the newcomers from Spain. They had expected friendly Indians, a settlement already in place, and gold at hand to collect for easy fortunes. There would be a lot of work ahead.

Columbus quickly chose a place for a new settlement, which he named Isabela. He did not choose wisely, however. There was no source of fresh water and the area was infested by mosquitoes.

About 20 men were sent to search for gold on the island. When they returned to Isabela two weeks later, nearly 300 of the settlers

One of the members of Christopher Columbus's second expedition to the New World was a young soldier named Juan Ponce de León. Ponce would eventually gain fame for exploring Puerto Rico and Florida.

were sick. Some of them had *malaria*, a disease that is carried by mosquitoes. Malaria causes severe fever and chills, and can be fatal. Food supplies were running low, and the men had not yet started planting crops.

Columbus had to send 12 ships back to Spain, asking Ferdinand and Isabella for more supplies. He reported that although there was illness, things were going well and that the explorers had found gold in the streams. This was not true. Columbus and several hundred men had spent a month searching the island for a gold mine without success.

As it became apparent that the search for a gold mine was a failure, Columbus ordered 50 men to build a fort, which he called San Tomas. Meanwhile, Columbus returned to Isabela. There, he found that the Spanish settlers were out of control. Some of the men disobeyed his orders, terrorizing the Indians. Although Columbus arrested several troublemakers, he could not stop the Spaniards' unrest.

Although Christopher Columbus was a brave sailor, he was not a good leader. Columbus was always happiest when he was sailing. He left his brother, Diego, in charge of Isabela and sailed to find new islands. For eight weeks, Columbus and his

*This picture shows Columbus checking his position on land with a tool called an astrolabe. This device was used by sailors to determine their north-south position (this is called **latitude**). Columbus was an expert sailor, but he was less skilled when it came to dealing with the people who settled in his colony.*

men explored Cuba. Even though they did not find the kingdom of the Grand Khan, Columbus insisted that the island was part of Cathay.

However, during Columbus's absence things had gotten worse at Isabela. The Spaniards and Indians were at war. Columbus couldn't stop his own men from fighting. He decided that the only way to end the war was to conquer the Indians. Although there were more Indians than Spaniards, they were afraid of the Europeans's weapons, horses, and dogs. One large battle was fought, but the natives ran away. The Spanish soldiers enslaved the Indians who remained, even though Ferdinand and Isabella had forbidden slavery. Some were put to work in the fields. Others were required to find a certain amount of gold every three months and give it to Columbus.

By the end of the year, many of the Indians on Hispaniola had died. Some were killed in battle; others died at the hands of cruel masters. But most had been killed by diseases like smallpox, measles, and typhoid fever. These diseases had been common in Europe. However, they were unknown in the New World until the Spaniards arrived. Because the natives had never been exposed to smallpox and other diseases, they did not have any *immunity*, or natural protection, against them.

Some of the Spaniards on Hispaniola were unhappy. One rebellious group took three caravels and sailed back to Spain. The rebels told Ferdinand and Isabella about the way Columbus had mishandled the colony. Their reports upset the king and queen. They sent for Columbus.

The Admiral left for Spain in March 1496. He traveled on the *Niña*, which was accompanied by another caravel. The ships, which normally would have carried about 50 men each, were crowded with 225 Spaniards anxious to leave. Food was very limited on the voyage. By the time the caravels arrived in Spain in June, the passengers were as thin as skeletons.

When Columbus met with Ferdinand and Isabella, he read them a list of 700 new islands he had discovered. In response, they asked what value these islands were to Spain if they held no spices or precious metals. Although the king and queen were not sure what Columbus had found, they were beginning to realize that it was not the Indies. Also, the disturbing reports from Hispaniola had made them aware that Columbus was not good at being governor. People at court began teasing Columbus, calling him Admiral of the Mosquitoes.

Columbus believed God was not pleased with him because he had displayed so much pride after his first voyage. To make up for it, he put on the plain brown robe and knotted rope belt worn by monks. He continued to dress that way for the rest of his life. The king and queen asked him to retire, but he refused. Columbus regarded the islands he had found as his property. He was not willing to give up control for a comfortable life in Spain.

The Search for
Redemption

By the year 1500, Christopher Columbus's life hit a new low point. Just seven years after his triumphant return to Spain as the discoverer of the Indies, he was brought back to Spain as a prisoner in chains.

6

wo years passed before Columbus received permission to make another voyage. Then, Ferdinand and Isabella learned from spies in Portugal that King Manõel, who had succeeded João II, believed there was a southern continent west of Africa in the Ocean Sea. He was going to send men to search for it. If the Portuguese found this land, they could threaten the colony in Hispaniola and Spain's control over the region.

Columbus was eager to explore to the south. Ancient scholars had believed gold could be found near the **equator**, an imaginary east-west line that divides the earth into two **hemispheres**.

The Admiral was also ordered to deliver 300 colonists to Hispaniola. It was difficult to find people who would go to the island, so recruits were found in the jails. Also, for the first time women were among the passengers when Columbus's six ships left Spain in May 1498.

The three ships carrying colonists sailed directly to Hispaniola. Columbus took the others south, landing on a large island with three large mountains. He named it Trinidad (Trinity). Next, he found a bay with large rivers emptying into it. Eventually, the Admiral realized that so much fresh water could not come from an island. It must be flowing from a huge land mass—a continent.

Since this continent's location did not fit into his picture of earth's geography, Columbus decided that he must be near a place described in the Bible: the Garden of Eden. He wrote, "Our Lord made the earthly paradise and in it placed the Tree of Life, and from it issues a fountain from which flow four of the chief rivers of this world . . . all the learned theologians agree that the earthly paradise is in the East." He had actually found South America.

Columbus now returned to Hispaniola. In his absence, he had instructed his brother Bartholomeo to move the settlement to a better location. The new town, Santo Domingo, was located at the mouth of a river. Unlike Isabela, it did not have a mosquito problem. However, there were other problems in Santo Domingo. An official of the colony named Francisco Roldán had led a rebellion. Some people remained loyal to Columbus, but others supported the rebels.

When the Spanish monarchs read a letter from Columbus telling them that he had found the Garden of Eden, they thought he had lost his mind. In the letter, Columbus also asked to have a wise and fair government official sent to Santo Domingo. He even offered to pay the man personally. Ferdinand and Isabella chose a trusted officer, Francisco de Bobadilla. But instead of sending him to help Columbus, they ordered Bobadilla to take control of the colony.

Upon his arrival at Santo Domingo, the first thing Bobadilla saw were corpses hanging from a *gallows*. He learned that five more Spanish rebels were to be hanged the next day. The governor and his brother Bartholomeo were out in the country-side, capturing rebels and sending them back to their brother Diego in town.

Bobadilla immediately arrested the three Columbus brothers and seized their belongings. In October of 1500 he sent them back to Spain in chains.

During the voyage, the captain of the ship offered to remove the **manacles**. Columbus refused, saying that only the king and queen had the power to release him. In Spain, he took refuge in a monastery. Ferdinand and Isabella soon ordered the chains to be removed, but Columbus kept them with him for the rest of his life. He even asked to have them buried with him.

Columbus met with Ferdinand and Isabella in December. He was now almost 50, an old man by the standards of that time. Hardships and illness had aged him even more. The king and queen listened to Columbus's accusations against Bobadilla, and his demand for the return of all the titles, property, and privileges that had been his.

In September 1501, Ferdinand and Isabella asked Bobadilla to return to Spain. They chose Nicolás de Ovando to be **adelantado**, or governor, of Hispaniola. Columbus was allowed to keep his

Columbus, in chains, pleads his case before the Queen.
Although she ordered his manacles to be removed, the
sailor kept the chains as a reminder of his humiliation.

titles, but he would never again have power on the island. In fact, he was ordered to stay away from Hispaniola. A trusted friend was sent on Columbus's behalf to try to get his gold from Hispaniola.

The king and queen offered Columbus a generous retirement income and a castle in Andalusia. Instead of accepting, Columbus pestered Ferdinand and Isabella to let him explore the regions that he had found on the third voyage. The king and queen finally agreed to his request. They provided four small ships for what would prove to be Christopher Columbus's final journey.

The fourth voyage, like the first, was entirely one of exploration. The historian Bartolomé Las Casas reported that Columbus wanted to take along Arabic translators "because he always held the opinion that . . . he had to come across people of the Grand Khan or others who spoke that language."

Columbus was no longer able to attract the best sailors of southern Spain. Most of the crew members were quite young, between 12 and 18 years of age. One of them was 12-year-old Ferdinand Columbus.

Columbus's four caravels left Spain on May 9, 1502. Columbus first sailed to Hispaniola, even though he had been told to stay away. One of his ships was damaged, and he wanted to replace it. As he neared the island, he saw signs that a hurricane was brewing. Governor Ovando was about to send a fleet off to Spain, so Columbus warned him about the storm. He also asked for permission to enter the port. The governor refused, so Columbus took his ships to a safe harbor nearby.

When the hurricane struck, 25 of Ovando's ships sank. Among the 500 men who drowned were

Columbus's enemies Bobadilla and Roldán. The only ship of the fleet to return to Spain was the one carrying Columbus's gold, which his friend had gotten for him.

Even after the storm, Ovando refused to allow Columbus to land. The Admiral sailed on, searching for the land of the Grand Khan. His fleet explored the coasts of present-day Honduras, Nicaragua, Costa Rica, and Panama without success. The ships were full of *shipworms* (clams that burrow into and eat away at submerged wood). They were leaky and sailed poorly. One ship was trapped on a sandbar and had to be abandoned.

Things grew worse when Columbus became sick with malaria. He thought of returning to Hispaniola, but one of his ships sank. The other two needed to be constantly bailed out to stay afloat. Columbus sailed to the nearest island, Jamaica, and had the ships deliberately run aground on the beach. "My vessel," he wrote, "was on the very point of sinking when our Lord miraculously brought us upon land."

Columbus and his sailors lived on Jamaica for a year. There was no way off the remote island without help. Fortunately, the Indians were friendly at first. Columbus borrowed several canoes and sent some of his crew to Hispaniola for help. It was a long, dangerous trip in the small wooden canoes. The sailors had to paddle 108 miles to reach the Spanish colony.

Things weren't much better for the men who stayed behind, either. Relations between the islanders and Columbus's men eventually broke down. Finally in June 1504, Governor Ovando sent a rescue ship from Hispaniola.

Columbus returned to Spain in November 1504. His royal **patron**, Queen Isabella, was ill when he returned. She died within a few weeks.

Columbus was a wealthy man, but he was bitter. He felt he had been mistreated by the king and queen. Now the seas were crowded with explorers—some were men who had sailed with him on earlier voyages—and he was forgotten.

Crippled with arthritis that was so bad he could barely move, Christopher Columbus died at age 55 on May 20, 1506, in Valladolid, Spain. His sons and a few close friends were with him.

Centuries passed before Columbus received credit for his accomplishment. He never realized that he had not found the Indies. However, the same determination that made him insist that he had dis-

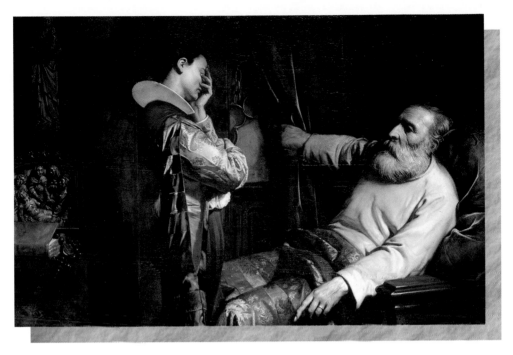

*In this painting of Columbus on his deathbed, the bitter
sailor shows his son the humiliating chains he was forced
to wear on his return to Spain in 1500.*

covered Cathay had driven him to make his voyage
of exploration in the first place, and kept him going
back. There are people who prefer the hardships of
exploration to a life of comfort and ease. Columbus
was one of them.

The title he most loved, Admiral of the Ocean
Sea, suits him very well. Sailing that unknown sea,
with skill and courage to match his conviction, he
was in his element. There, he was a truly great
explorer.

Chronology

1419 Prince Henry the Navigator launches the era of Portuguese exploration.

1451 Christopher Columbus is born in Genoa, Italy.

1469 Ferdinand of Aragon marries Isabella of Castile; together, they unite Spain.

1476 Columbus goes to Lisbon, Portugal.

1479 Columbus marries Felipa Perestrello e Moniz.

1484 The King of Portugal refuses to finance Columbus's proposed sea voyage to the Indies; Felipa dies; Columbus goes to Spain.

1486 Columbus tries to convince Ferdinand and Isabella to sponsor his expedition.

1487 Sailing for Portugal, Bartholomeo Dias rounds the tip of Africa.

1492 Ferdinand and Isabella decide to sponsor Columbus; Columbus leaves August 3 to make his first voyage across the unknown waters of the Ocean Sea; lands on the island of San Salvador on October 12; explores islands, including Cuba and Hispaniola, until December.

1493 Columbus returns to Spain, where he is hailed as a hero.

1493 Makes a second voyage, during which Columbus discovers many islands and establishes a permanent Spanish colony on Hispaniola. Many of the native Indians are killed or enslaved.

1497 Columbus leaves Spain for his third voyage; discovers Trinidad and the South American continent.

1500 Unable to govern Hispaniola, Columbus is sent back to Spain in chains in October.

1502 Columbus begins his fourth, and final, voyage. He is refused entry at Hispaniola, and spends a year shipwrecked on Jamaica.

1504 Columbus returns to Spain; Queen Isabella dies in December.

1506 Columbus dies on May 20 in Valladolid, Spain.

Glossary

adelantado–the title of a Spanish governor in the New World.

caravel–a sturdy sailing ship developed by the Portuguese. Caravels had broad hulls, a high and narrow deck at the stern (called a "poop deck"), and three masts.

Capitulations–the agreement between Columbus and the king and queen of Spain.

coat of arms–a symbolic emblem that depicts a person's heritage or accomplishments.

coral reefs–large, hard underwater ridges made up of the stony skeletons of sea creatures called coral.

equator–an imaginary east-west line that divides the earth into two equal parts, the Northern and Southern hemispheres.

flagship–a ship that carries the commander of a fleet.

gallows–a frame from which criminals are hanged.

geography–the study of the earth's form, and its division into land and sea areas.

heathen–an uncivilized person, or (to Columbus) any person who was not Christian.

hemisphere–half of the earth.

hereditary–describes property that is passed from generation to generation.

hull–the main frame and body of a ship, not including the masts, sails, or rigging.

immunity–natural protection from disease. Native Americans were not immune to diseases carried by Europeans, and so faced a greater risk of dying from the diseases.

latitude–a measure of distance north or south of the equator.

malaria–a blood disease carried by mosquitoes that causes severe chills and fever and was often fatal.

manacles–chains or handcuffs.

monastery–a settlement of people (often called monks) who have dedicated themselves to religion.

mutiny–a revolt by a ship's crew against discipline or against a commanding officer.

nautical mile–a measurement of distance over the ocean. At 6,076 feet, it is longer than a regular mile (5,280 feet).

navigation–the science of directing the course of a seagoing vessel, and of determining its position.

Ocean Sea–a 15th century name for the Atlantic Ocean.

patron–a person who uses his or her wealth and power to help someone else.

pitch–a thick, black, flammable substance made from boiling tar.

provisions–a stock of food and water.

rector–the clergyman who is in charge of a monastery.

Sargasso Sea–a large area of the mid-Atlantic where seaweed floats on top of the water.

shipworms–small clams that damage submerged wood.

spices–any of various aromatic vegetable products, such as pepper or nutmeg, used to season or flavor foods. Spices were rare and highly valued by the people of Europe.

trade winds–strong northeasterly winds that helped Columbus's ships cross the Atlantic.

Further Reading

Brenner, Barbara. *If You Were There In 1492*. New York: Aladdin Paperbacks, 1998.

Columbus, Christopher, and Antonio Pigafetta. *To America and Around the World: The Logs of Christopher Columbus and of Ferdinand Magellan*. Boston: Branden Publishing, 1991.

Dodge, Stephen C., *Christopher Columbus and the First Voyages to the New World*. New York: Chelsea House Publishers, 1991.

Dor-Ner, Zvi. *Columbus and the Age of Discovery*. New York: William Morrow, 1992.

Fritz, Jean. *Where Do You Think You're Going, Christopher Columbus?* New York: G. P. Putnam's Sons, 1997.

Hynson, Colin. *Columbus and the Renaissance Explorers*. Hauppauge, N.Y.: Barron's Educational Series, Inc., 1998.

Mason, Antony, and Keith Lye. *The Children's Atlas of Exploration: Follow in the Footsteps of the Great Explorers*. Brookfield, CT: Millbrook Press, 1993.

Sis, Peter. *Follow the Dream*. New York: Dragonfly, 1996.

Stefoff, Rebecca. *Vasco da Gama and the Portuguese Explorers*. New York: Chelsea House Publishers, 1993.

Yolen, Jane. *Encounter*. New York: Harcourt Brace & Co., 1996.

Index

Picture Credits

As a mother of four, **CAROLE S. GALLAGHER** spent many hours reading to, and with, her children. In 1998, she earned her BA in English from Wilson College, after balancing family, job, and school for several years. She believes that children need to learn about the past in order to understand the present and, someday, to shape the future. *Christopher Columbus and the Discovery of the New World* is her first book.